HAWAI*with* SPAM®

MINI EDITION

by
Muriel Miura

MUTUAL PUBLISHING

Hawai'i Cooks with Spam (Mini Edition)
  © 2018 by Mutual Publishing
Hawai'i Cooks with Spam (Original Edition)
  © 2008 by Mutual Publishing

The information contained in this
book is accurate and complete to the
best of our knowledge. All recipes and
recommendations are made without
guarantees. The author and publisher
disclaim all liabilities in connection with the
use of the information contained within.

Library of Congress Control Number:
2018940684

ISBN-13: 978-1939487-90-2

Food styling by Hideaki Miyoshi
Photography by Kaz Tanabe
Cover photographs from Dreamstime.com:
  musubi © Bhofack2, background ©
  Panamae
First Printing, August 2018

Mutual Publishing, LLC
1215 Center Street, Suite 210
Honolulu, Hawai'i 96816
Ph: 808-732-1709 / Fax: 808-734-4094
info@mutualpublishing.com
www.mutualpublishing.com

Printed in China

CONTENTS

INTRODUCTION

SPAM®, a family of tasty and pre-cooked luncheon meats, is a product of Hormel Foods Corporation (formerly Hormel & Company). Eleven years after introducing the first canned ham in 1926, Jay C. Hormel, son of the company's founder, determined to find a use for surplus pork shoulder, developed a distinctive canned blend of chopped pork known as Hormel® spiced ham that didn't require refrigeration. The Austin, Minnesota-based Hormel Company sponsored a contest to find a name that was unique to this new product and the winning entry, SPAM®, was submitted by Kenneth Daigneau, an actor from New York and brother of a Hormel vice present. He won $100 for naming this great tasting, convenient, and moderately priced luncheon meat.

Through more than eight decades, SPAM® has remained Hawai'i's favorite canned meat. It is a contemporary product known for its versatility, quality, great taste, and convenience. The SPAM® Family of Products are fully cooked, ready-to-eat, and have a good shelf life. They are used to flavor many dishes and are delicious with rice, noodles, and vegetables—and especially great for musubi and Island-style plate lunches!

Many of these recipes are treasured ones from friends, family, and fans. They are all the result of years of sharing the fun of cooking. You'll find that there is no limit to food horizons with SPAM®. Use these recipes as a guide to create some of your own, and enjoy. Whatever the reason or season, the SPAM® Cookbook will help you provide the perfect dish—simple or fancy—for any meal or occasion. Let's eat SPAM®!

THE SECRET TO BEING A SUCCESSFUL COOK

1. Read recipe from beginning to end first. Make sure you understand what you're supposed to do.
2. Make certain that you have all the ingredients needed for the chosen recipe.
3. Gather all the necessary equipment before you begin.
4. Measure the ingredients accurately.
5. Practice good kitchen and food safety habits.
6. When done, put all the ingredients and equipment away. Wash and dry all the dirty dishes and make sure that the kitchen is clean and neat.

ABOUT SPAM® CLASSIC

Hailed as the "miracle meat," SPAM® attracted the attention of the United States military during World War II for its shelf-stable attributes, and by 1940 most Americans overseas had gotten a taste of it. Our allies were enjoying SPAM® soon after. Since fresh meat was difficult to get, surpluses of SPAM® from the soldiers made their way into Hawai'i's diets as well as those of other Pacific islands…the rest is history. SPAM® remains a part of Hawai'i's culture today, and Hawai'i is the leading consumer of SPAM® in the United States with more than six milliion cans per year, or six cans per person per year consumed. According to Hormel Foods, more than six billion cans of SPAM® were produced by 2002. Amazing, isn't it?

Because of its versatility and unique flavor, SPAM® is used in a variety of ways, such as sandwich meats, salad ingredients, sushi filling, musubi toppings, or to make a meaty macaroni and cheese. It is served or cooked with cheese, eggs, pineapples; it is sliced, diced, chopped, grated. Hot or cold, baked or fried—the combinations are endless. In keeping with Hawai'i's tradition of ethnic foods, the recipes in this book reflect the cultural influences of various countries.

NUTRITION FACTS*

Nutrition Facts for SPAM® 25% Less Sodium:
Serving Size: 2 oz. (56 g)   Servings per Container: 6
Calories: 180   Fat Calories: 140

Amount/serving	%DV★	Amount/serving	%DV★
Total Fat 16 g	25%	Total Carb. 1 g	0%
Sat. Fat 6 g	30%	Fiber 0 g	0%
Cholest. 40 mg	13%	Sugars 0 g	0%
Sodium 580 mg	24%	Protein 7 g	
Vitamin A	0%	Vitamin C	30%
Calcium	0%	Iron	2%

Percent Daily Values (DV) based on 2,000-calorie diet. Nutritional data subject to change based on type of SPAM®; data available on each can.

SPAM® PREPARATION TECHNIQUES FOR RECIPES

1. **Slice:** Cut lengthwise into 8 to 10 slices per can.
2. **Chop:** Cut into cubes.
3. **Mince:** Cut into very small pieces.
4. **Grate:** Use large holes of a grater.
5. **Ground:** Use small holes of a grater.
6. **Sticks** or **Strips:** Cut into 8 to 10 lengthwise slices then cut crosswise or lengthwise again, depending upon the length desired. If thicker sticks or strips are desired, initially cut into fewer slices.
7. **Mash:** Use potato masher.

A can of any of the SPAM® Family of Products called for in recipes, refers to a 12-ounce can. Unless otherwise stated, **SPAM® with 25% less sodium** is used for the recipes in this book.

Any type of SPAM® may be used for any of the recipes, however, the seasonings may need to be adjusted to your taste.

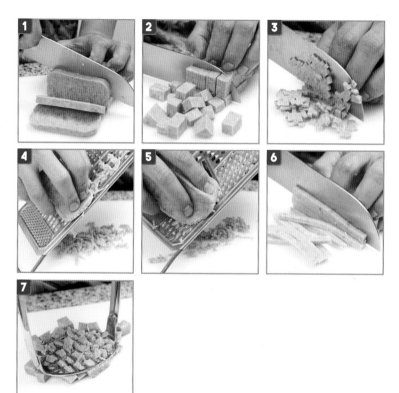

SPAM™ CLASSIC RECIPE

Makes 4 servings

Going back to the beginning, I'd like to share the original Baked SPAM® recipe which appeared on the familiar blue-and-yellow cans until 1977. It was also the first of many SPAM™ recipes that I've collected over the years:

1 (12 oz.) can classic SPAM®
   25% Less Sodium or any variety
Whole cloves
⅓ cup packed brown sugar
1 teaspoon water
1 teaspoon prepared mustard
½ teaspoon vinegar

Place SPAM® on rack in shallow baking pan. Score surface and stud with cloves. In small bowl, combine brown sugar, water, mustard, and vinegar, stirring until smooth. Brush glaze over SPAM®. Bake 20 minutes at 375°F, basting often. Cut into slices.

Variation:
- **Baked Pineapple SPAM®:** Combine ¼ cup brown sugar and ½ cup pineapple juice or crushed pineapple; stir to combine. Spread over top and sides of SPAM® loaf. Place in oven and bake at 350°F for 30 to 40 minutes.

ISLAND
FAVORITES

ISLAND SPAM®

Makes 4 servings

This recipe is from Hawai'i's SPAM JAM®, which is held annually in Waikīkī.

1 can SPAM® Classic (12 ounces), cubed
1 chopped onion
1 clove chopped garlic
1½ cups water
1 cup uncooked white rice
1 tablespoon chopped parsley
1 bay leaf, finely crushed
¼ teaspoon pepper
Ground red pepper

In large skillet, lightly brown SPAM®, onion, and garlic. Stir in all remaining ingredients, except red pepper; bring to a boil. Reduce heat and simmer, covered, 15 minutes or until rice is cooked. Sprinkle with red pepper before serving.

SPAM™ OMELET

Makes about 2 servings

⅓ cup minced SPAM®
2 tablespoons chopped onion
1 tablespoon salad oil
2 tablespoons minced green onion
4 eggs, beaten

Stir-fry SPAM® and onion in hot oil in skillet or omelet pan about 30 seconds. Pour eggs and green onion into pan and stir with fork to spread eggs continuously over bottom of pan as they thicken. Let stand over heat a few seconds to brown bottom of omelet lightly. Tilt pan, run fork under edge of omelet, then jerk skillet sharply to loosen eggs from bottom of skillet. Fold portion of omelet just to center; turn omelet onto plate, flipping folded portion of omelet so it rolls over the bottom. Serve with soy sauce or catsup, if desired.

SPAM® 'N EGGS

Makes 2 servings

1 can SPAM®, cut into 4 lengthwise slices
4 eggs, cooked as desired

Pan-fry SPAM® slices in nonstick skillet until golden brown and crisp on both sides; drain on absorbent paper and set aside. Meanwhile, cook eggs as desired and serve with two scoops of hot steamed rice or hash brown potatoes. 'Ono with soy sauce or catsup over everything!

Variation:
- **SPAM™- Loco Moco:** Arrange rice, SPAM®, and eggs in layers; pour your favorite brown gravy over eggs and serve with side of your favorite macaroni salad.

SAIMIN WITH SPAM®

Makes about 2 servings

1 package (9.5 ounces) fresh saimin

Broth:
4 cups water
2½ teaspoons dashi-no-moto (fish broth powder)
¼ cup soy sauce
3 tablespoons mirin (sweet rice wine)

Condiments:
Fried egg strips
¼ cup SPAM® strips
6 slices kamaboko (fishcake)
Minced green onion
Kizami nori (shredded seaweed)

Cook saimin as directed on package. Rinse and drain. To make Broth, combine water, dashi-no-moto, soy sauce, and mirin; bring to a boil. Place cooked noodles in individual bowls, cover with broth, and sprinkle with desired condiments. Serve with Mustard-Soy Sauce (see page 21).

SPAM™ TERIYAKI

Makes 3 to 4 servings

¼ cup soy sauce
¼ cup sugar
¼ cup mirin (sweet rice wine)
2 tablespoons water
1 can SPAM® classic, sliced

Combine soy sauce, sugar, mirin, and water in skillet; bring to a boil. Add SPAM® slices and cook over medium heat 2 to 3 minutes. Drain and serve with hot steamed rice or use as topping for SPAM™ Teriyaki Musubi (see page 25).

CRISPY SPAM™ WON TON *(Fried Dumplings)*

Makes about 50

Filling:
1 can SPAM®, finely minced
½ pound lean ground pork
8 canned water chestnuts, minced
4 stalks green onion, chopped
1 egg, beaten
1 tablespoon soy sauce
1 teaspoon sugar

1 package (50 count) won ton wrappers
1 quart canola oil for frying

Mustard-Soy Sauce:
2 teaspoons dry mustard
2 teaspoons water
2 to 3 tablespoons soy sauce

Combine Filling ingredients; toss to mix well. Fill each won ton wrapper with a generous teaspoonful of Filling mixture. Moisten edge of won ton wrapper with water and press firmly together into desired shapes (triangle, rectangle, or fancy). Deep-fry in oil heated to 365°F until golden brown, turning once. Drain on absorbent paper. Serve with Sweet-Sour Sauce (see page 56) or Mustard-Soy Sauce.

To prepare Mustard-Soy Sauce, combine all ingredients and mix until smooth

CLASSIC SPAM™ MUSUBI

Makes 8 musubi

The first SPAM™ musubi I had was made very simply, but I remember it to be sooooo delicious! For those who like simple things, following is the "classic" version.

1 can SPAM®, sliced into 8 lengthwise pieces
4 cups cooked short grain rice
4 sheets nori, cut in half

Fry SPAM® in hot nonstick skillet until browned and a little crisp; set aside. Lay piece of nori flat on work surface and center acrylic SPAM® musubi mold on top of nori. Fill mold with rice and press down firmly. Place SPAM® on top of rice and fold nori over SPAM® and seal. Cool; may be cut in half and wrapped in waxed paper or plastic wrap, if desired.

TSUKUDANI
SPAM™ MUSUBI

Makes 16 musubi

This variation was developed by David Hisashima, a courtroom deputy at U.S. District Court. It's easy to make and really 'ono!

2 cans SPAM®, sliced into 16 lengthwise pieces
1 cup prepared teriyaki sauce, optional
7½ cups cooked short grain rice
8 sheets nori, cut in half
1 bottle (1.5 ounces) furikake (seasoned Japanese seaweed mix)
1 bottle (3.3 ounces) tsukudani nori (flavored seaweed paste; available at Asian markets and Oriental food sections of markets.)

Fry SPAM® in hot nonstick skillet until lightly browned. Brush with teriyaki sauce; set aside. Mix rice with furikake.

Lay a piece of nori flat on work surface. Place SPAM™ musubi mold over center of nori. Fill mold half-way with rice. Spread paste over rice and top with SPAM®. Fill mold with more rice; press down firmly. Remove mold; fold nori over SPAM® and press to seal. Wrap in plastic wrap, if desired.

Variations:

- **SPAM™ Teriyaki Musubi:** Cook SPAM® slices in ¼ cup each of soy sauce, mirin, and sugar for 1 to 2 minutes. Drain well before placing on rice; fold nori over SPAM® and press to seal.

- **Korean-Style SPAM™ Musubi:** Toss cooked rice with 1 teaspoon toasted sesame seeds and 1 tablespoon sesame-chili oil; mix well. Place well-drained chopped cabbage kim chee (Korean pickle) on rice before placing SPAM® on rice; fold nori over SPAM® and press to seal.

- **Furikake SPAM™ Musubi:** Omit nori paste (tsukudani); proceed as directed.

- **SPAM™ Omelet Musubi:** Scramble 2 to 3 large eggs with 1 teaspoon soy sauce; cook in hot oil in skillet until well done; slice to fit musubi mold. Sprinkle furikake over rice before topping with egg, followed by slice of SPAM®. Fold nori over SPAM® and press to seal.

BROILED SPAM™ NIGIRI

Makes 24 pieces

4 cups cooked short grain rice, cooled to room temperature
⅓ cup Nori Komi Furikake (sesame seed and seaweed seasoning)
6 dried shiitake mushrooms, soaked in warm water and minced
1 can SPAM®, finely chopped
¾ cup sour cream
½ cup mayonnaise
2 packages (0.19 ounce each) Korean nori (seasoned seaweed)

Spread rice in 9 × 3 × 13-inch pan; sprinkle furikake evenly over rice; set aside. Mix together mushrooms, SPAM®, sour cream, and mayonnaise; spread mixture evenly over furikake layer. Broil 5 to 6 minutes or until light brown. Cool; cut into 24 pieces. Wrap each piece in sheet of Korean nori to serve.

CLASSIC & ETHNIC FAVORITES

SPAM™ BREAKFAST BAKE

Makes about 6 servings

6 slices bread, torn into bite-size pieces
½ can SPAM®, cut into bite-size pieces
½ cup shredded cheese (cheddar, Monterey Jack, jalapeño, Swiss, or American)
6 eggs, beaten slightly
1¼ cup milk
Dash pepper

Sprinkle half of bread pieces into bottom of greased 2-quart baking dish. Sprinkle SPAM® and cheese over bread; sprinkle remaining bread cubes over SPAM® and cheese. Beat together eggs, milk, and pepper until well mixed; pour mixture over bread layers. Cover with plastic wrap; chill in refrigerator 2 hours or longer. Remove plastic wrap and bake at 325°F 30 to 35 minutes or until table knife inserted in center of food comes out clean. Cool 10 minutes and cut into squares to serve.

SPAMWICH™ SANDWICHES

Makes 4 sandwiches

1 can SPAM®
8 slices bread of choice (whole wheat, 7-grain, etc.)
Mayonnaise
Catsup, optional

Cut SPAM® into eight ¼-inch thick lengthwise slices; pan-fry SPAM® in nonstick skillet 1 to 2 minutes; drain on absorbent paper. (It is not necessary to cook SPAM®; it may be served cold straight from the can.) Spread mayonnaise on one side of bread slices; arrange 2 slices of SPAM® on each slice of bread. Spread catsup or sauce of choice on SPAM®, if desired. Top with lettuce or other condiments, then another slice of bread.

Variations:

- **SPAM® 'n Cheese Sandwiches:** Add a slice of cheese (Swiss or cheddar).
- **Barbecued SPAMWICH™ Sandwiches:** Use purchased barbecue sauce instead of mayonnaise.
- **Grilled Cheese 'n SPAM®:** Butter bread slices. Place SPAM® slices on unbuttered side and top with American cheese and another slice of bread; brown on both sides in hot skillet sprayed with butter or oil until brown.

- **SPAM® 'n Egg Sandwiches:** Add egg, cooked as desired, and place on top of SPAM®.
- **SPAM™ Dagwood Sandwiches:** On a slice of bread, stack a slice of SPAM®, cheese, then lettuce, another slice of bread, SPAM®, then slice of cooked turkey or chicken, lettuce and tomato topped with another slice of bread. Use spread of choice on bread slices.
- **And More...**Use other types of breads (Hoagie, onion, sesame seed, French, Kaiser, croissant, etc.)

SPAM®
AND PEA SALAD

Makes 2 to 4 servings

1 package (16 ounces)
   frozen peas
½ cup minced SPAM®
¼ cup minced onion
⅓ cup mayonnaise
Salt and pepper to taste

Cook peas according to package directions. Drain well and chill 2 to 4 hours; mix with remaining ingredients and adjust taste as necessary. Serve on a bed of lettuce.

MAC 'N CHEESE WITH SPAM®

Makes 2 to 4 servings

This tops the list for lunch or a heavy snack for my grandchildren. Add 1 cup of frozen veggies to make this a meal-in-one!

1 box (7¼ ounces) macaroni
   and cheese
½ can SPAM®, cubed
Grated cheddar cheese,
   optional

Prepare macaroni and cheese according to package directions. Place mixture in casserole; add SPAM® and sprinkle top with additional cheddar cheese, if desired. Bake at 350°F for 25 to 30 minutes or until top is golden brown.

ALL-AMERICAN

ALL-AMERICAN

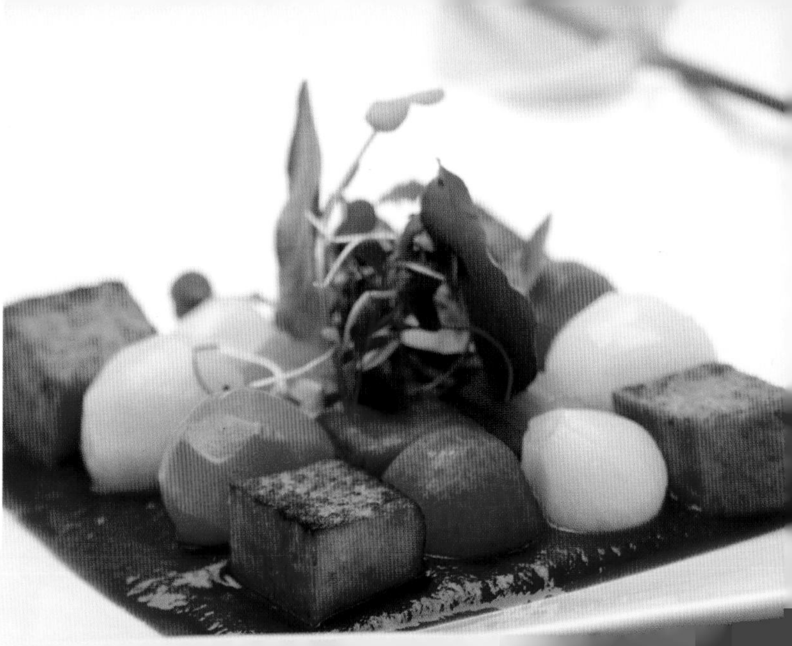

BROKE DA MOUTH SPAM™ STEW

Makes 6 to 8 servings

I remember this favorite concoction of some of the Hawai'i students living in dorms during the fifties.

3 cans SPAM®, cut into large
   cubes
½ cup flour
¼ cup salad oil
2 medium onions, wedged
5 cups water
2 bay leaves
1½ teaspoons salt
¼ teaspoon pepper
2 cans (8 ounces each) tomato
   sauce
4 small carrots, cut into 1-inch
   pieces
4 small potatoes, pared and
   quartered
1 cup sliced celery

Dredge SPAM® in flour; brown lightly on all sides in hot oil. Add onions and brown lightly. Add water and bay leaves; simmer 10 to 15 minutes over medium heat. Add remaining ingredients; simmer additional 20 to 25 minutes or until vegetables are done. Adjust taste as necessary.

SPAM™-STUFFED BAKED POTATOES

Makes 4 servings

4 medium baking potatoes
½ cup milk, scalded
¼ cup butter
¼ teaspoon salt
¼ cup grated onion
1 can SPAM®, shredded
Grated cheddar cheese

Bake potatoes at 450°F for 1 hour or until tender. Remove from the oven and let cool. Cut potatoes in half lengthwise; scoop flesh into bowl; save skins. Add milk, butter, salt, and onion to potato flesh; beat with hand mixer until creamy. Fold in SPAM®; spoon mixture into potato skins and top with grated cheese. Place stuffed potatoes in baking pan and bake at 400°F for 15 to 20 minutes or until heated through.

TROPICAL BAKED SPAM®

Makes 4 servings

I remember this recipe as one of the more "fancy" things I learned to prepare while taking home economics in junior high school. In those days, we were not as sophisticated as the teens of today.

1 can SPAM®
¼ cup brown sugar, packed
1 can (8¼ ounces)
   crushed pineapple
6 to 8 cloves

Cover top and sides of SPAM® with brown sugar and crushed pineapple. Stick cloves into SPAM® loaf and bake at 350°F for 30 to 40 minutes or until brown.

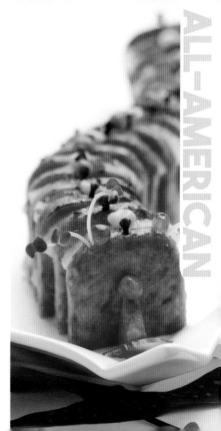

ALL-AMERICAN

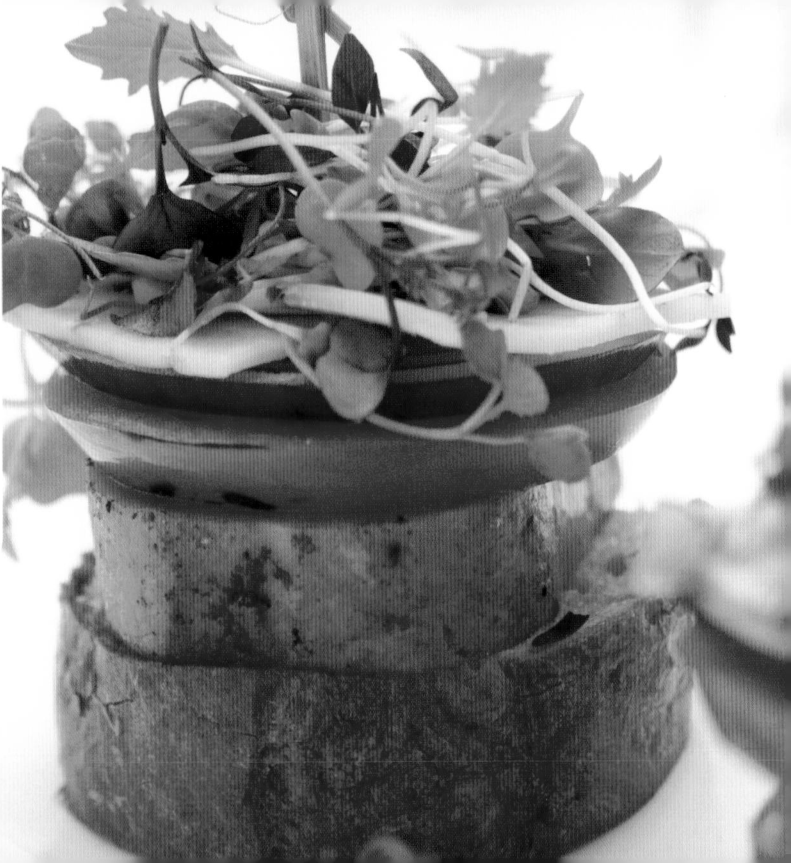

SPAMBURGER®

Makes 4 to 6 servings

2 cans SPAM®, finely chopped	**Suggested Condiments:**
½ cup minced onion	Prepared mustard
¼ cup bread crumbs	Mayonnaise
1 egg, beaten	Sweet pickle relish
	Sweet onion slices
	Tomato slices
	Lettuce

Combine SPAM®, onion, bread crumbs, and egg; mix well and shape into 1-inch thick patties. Pan-fry in hot skillet sprayed with vegetable oil or broil until browned on both sides. Drain on absorbent paper. Place each patty on split hamburger bun and top with desired condiments.

Variations:
- **Open-faced Burger:** Cut SPAM® into thick slices, pan fry, and place atop French bread slices.
- **SPAMBURGER® with Cheese:** Top burgers with cheese slices of choice while hot.
- **SPAMBurger™ Plate Lunch:** Pour prepared brown gravy over burger and serve with hot steamed rice and salad of choice (mo' 'ono with macaroni salad).

SPAM™ KATSU *(Breaded SPAM® Cutlet)*

Makes about 4 servings

1 can SPAM®, sliced into 8 pieces
1 egg, beaten
Panko or fine bread crumbs
Canola oil for frying

Katsu Sauce:
½ cup catsup
3 tablespoons Worcestershire
   sauce
Dash pepper
Liquid hot sauce to taste

Coat SPAM® slices with egg; dredge all surfaces in panko or bread crumbs. Pan-fry in hot oil in skillet until golden brown on both sides. Drain on absorbent paper and serve with Katsu Sauce.

To make Katsu Sauce, combine all ingredients; mix well. Serve as dip or drizzle over SPAM® Katsu.

Variation:
- **Curried SPAM™ Katsudon:** Place slices of SPAM™ Katsu over hot steamed rice in bowl. Pour prepared packaged curry sauce following directions on package.

KYURI-SPAM™ NAMASU
(Cucumber-SPAM® Salad)

Makes 3 to 4 servings

1 or 2 strips wakame (seaweed)
1 large cucumber, cut in half
   lengthwise and thinly sliced
1 tablespoon chopped carrots
⅓ cup chopped SPAM®

Sauce:
¼ cup sugar
¼ cup rice vinegar
1 tablespoon lemon juice
Pinch of salt, optional

Wash and soak wakame in warm water for 15 to 20 minutes; remove tough
center rib and cut into small pieces; set aside. Sprinkle salt over cucumber
slices; let stand 20 minutes; rinse and squeeze out excess liquid. Combine
wakame, vegetables, and SPAM® with Sauce ingredients; toss and chill
until ready to serve.

SOMEN–SPAM™ SALAD

Makes about 6 to 8 servings

½ package (8 ounce size)
  somen (thin noodles)
1 medium head lettuce, finely
  shredded
1 cup slivered kamaboko
  (fishcake)
1 cup thin SPAM® strips
½ cup fried egg strips
½ cup minced green onion
Teriyaki kizami nori (roasted
  shredded seaweed)

Dressing:
1 tablespoon toasted sesame
  seeds
1 tablespoon sugar
½ teaspoon salt
1½ tablespoons salad oil
2 tablespoons rice vinegar
1 tablespoon soy sauce

Cook somen according to package directions. Rinse, drain, and chill 30 minutes. Spread lettuce evenly on large platter. Wrap somen into small bundles and place on top of lettuce. Arrange kamaboko, SPAM®, fried egg strips, and green onion on somen. Sprinkle with nori. Combine Dressing ingredients; mix well and serve with Somen Salad.

SUSHI RICE

Makes 15 cups sushi rice

5 cups short grain rice
5¼ cups water

Vinegar Sauce:
1 cup rice vinegar
1 cup sugar
¼ cup mirin (sweet rice wine)
1 tablespoon salt

Wash rice and drain. Add water and let water come to a boil; reduce heat to simmer and cook 5 to 8 minutes or until water level is reduced to level of rice. Cook additional 7 to 8 minutes over low heat. Let steam, covered, 10 minutes before transferring to large non-reactive bowl or large shallow container.

Combine Vinegar Sauce ingredients; cook over medium heat until sugar dissolves; cool. Sprinkle half over hot rice and toss gently; add more sauce, if desired. Toss and fan rice to cool quickly. Use Sushi Rice in sushi of choice.

SPAM™ NORI MAKI SUSHI *(Sushi Roll)*

Makes 8 to 10 rolls

1 can (12 ounces) SPAM®, cut into ½-inch strips and fried
1 jar tsukudani nori (flavored seaweed paste)
10 cucumber sticks, length of sushi nori
10 sheets sushi nori (seaweed)
1 recipe sushi rice (see page 44)

Place sheet of nori on sudare (bamboo mat) and align with edge nearest you. Using hand moistened with rice vinegar, spread 1 cup sushi rice evenly over 5 × 8-inch area leaving 2 inches nori at far end bare. Using a spoon or knife, spread sushi rice surface with tsukudani nori. Arrange a cucumber stick 1 inch from edge nearest you followed by a SPAM® strip(s). Lift mat with thumbs; keep cucumber and meat in place with fingers, and roll mat over meat and away from you. When mat touches the rice, lift mat and continue to roll as you would for jelly roll. Roll again in mat and apply slight pressure to tighten roll. To serve, cut each roll into 7 or 8 pieces. Arrange sushi slices on platter, cut side up.

URAMAKI SPAM™ SUSHI
(Inside-Out Rolled Sushi)

Makes 8 to 10 rolls

1 recipe sushi rice (see page 44)
10 sheets sushi nori
20 pieces SPAM® strips
10 cucumber sticks, length of sushi nori
Mayonnaise
Wasabi paste
Tobiko (flying fish roe)

To roll sushi, place sushi rice on plastic wrap that is cut to the size of the sushi nori sheet or bamboo mat. Place sushi nori on top of rice. Arrange a row each of SPAM®, cucumber, mayonnaise, and wasabi paste about 1½ inches from nearest edge. Lift plastic wrap or mat with thumbs while keeping filling in place with fingers. Bring edge of plastic or mat over filling and roll away from you with palm, being careful not to encase plastic wrap or mat. Apply slight pressure to tighten roll then roll in tobiko. To serve, cut each roll in 7 or 8 pieces and place cut side up on plate. Dip in wasabi-soy sauce, if desired.

HAWAIIAN TEMAKI SPAM™ SUSHI
(SPAM™ Sushi Hand Roll)

Makes 10 rolls

5 sheets sushi nori, cut in half
2½ cups sushi rice (see page 44)
Wasabi paste
10 pieces SPAM® strips
10 cucumber strips, cut into 5-inch lengths
Radish sprouts
Soy sauce

Place a sheet of sushi nori in palm of hand and spoon about ¼ cup sushi rice over and spread evenly on nori. Place a streak of wasabi paste along center of rice and lay strips of SPAM®, cucumber, and radish sprouts. Wrap nori around filling, starting at lower end of nori and rolling diagonally into cone shape. Serve with soy sauce, if desired.

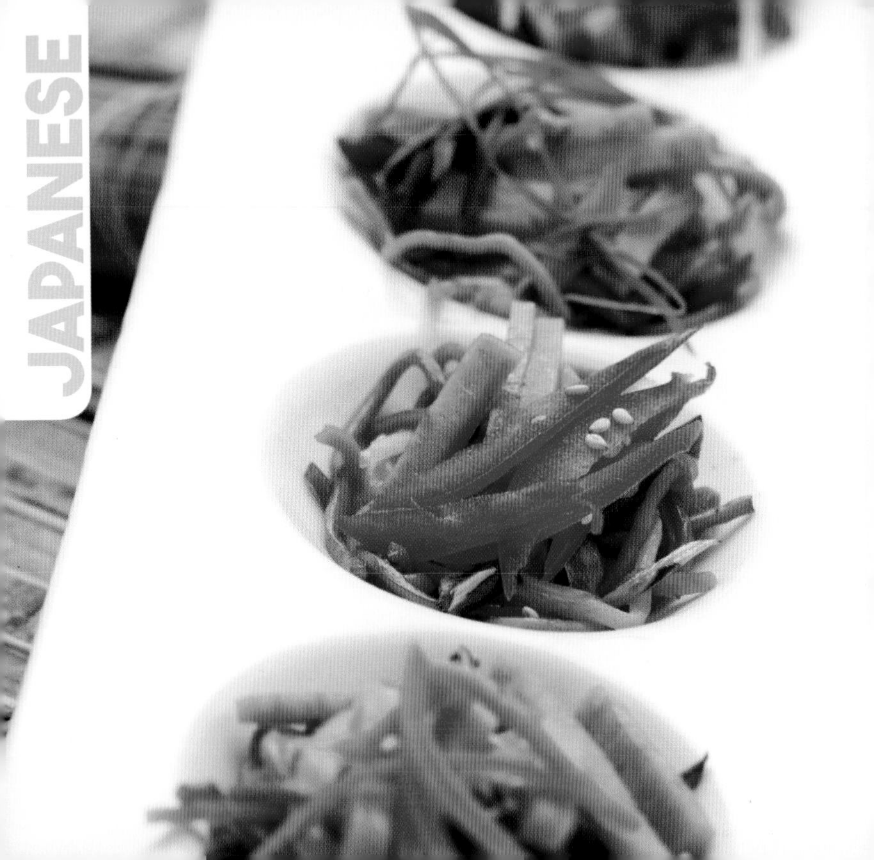
JAPANESE

SPAM™ YAKI SOBA *(Fried Noodles)*

Makes 4 to 6 servings

½ cup chopped SPAM®
1 teaspoon salad oil
1 small onion, sliced
2 cups bean sprouts
½ cup carrot, slivered
½ cup green onion, cut into
   1½-inch lengths
1 pound fresh ramen or yaki
   soba (wheat noodles)

Seasonings:
2 tablespoons soy sauce
3 tablespoons chicken broth
1 package (2½ teaspoons) dashi-
   no-moto (fish broth powder)

Garnishes:
SPAM® strips
2 tablespoons toasted sesame
   seeds
¼ cup minced green onion or
   Chinese parsley

Stir-fry SPAM® in hot oil 1 minute. Add vegetables, noodles, and seasonings; stir-fry additional minutes to heat through. Garnish with additional SPAM®, sesame seeds, and green onion or Chinese parsley before serving.

SPINY SPAM™ TEMPURA

Makes about 18 to 24

½ pound raw seasoned fishcake
½ cup minced SPAM®
½ cup flour
4 ounces somen (thin noodles), broken into ¾-inch lengths
1 quart salad oil for frying

Batter:
1 egg, slightly beaten
½ cup water
½ cup flour
½ cup cornstarch

Mix together fishcake and SPAM® and form into walnut-size balls. Dredge in flour and set aside. Add egg to water and beat to combine; add to flour and cornstarch mixture; stir until ingredients are blended together. Dip SPAM™ balls in batter; roll in somen. Deep-fry in oil heated to 365°F until golden brown. Drain on absorbent paper and serve hot.

SPAM™ TEMPURA *(Fritters)*

Makes 4 to 6 servings

1 can SPAM®, cut into ¼-inch thick strips
Sweet potato, peeled and julienne slices

Bell peppers, julienne
Green beans, French cut
Round onion slices
1 quart canola oil

Batter:
½ cup flour
½ cup cornstarch
1 egg, beaten
½ cup cold water

Tempura Sauce:
1 cup water
½ teaspoon dashi-no-moto (fish broth powder)
¼ cup mirin (sweet rice wine)
¼ cup soy sauce
1½ tablespoons sugar

To prepare batter, combine flour and cornstarch. Combine egg with cold water separately; stir to mix thoroughly. Add liquid to dry mixture all at once; stir only until flour mixture is moistened. Dip strips of SPAM® with a combination of any of the vegetables into the batter. Deep-fry in oil heated to 365°F until delicately browned. Drain on absorbent paper and serve hot with Tempura Sauce.

Combine all ingredients for Tempura Sauce in saucepan; bring to a boil; cool. If desired, add 1 tablespoon minced green onion or grated daikon just before serving.

SPAM™ CHOW FUN (*Stir-Fried Flat Noodles*)

Makes 6 to 8 servings

2 tablespoons salad oil
1 can SPAM®, slivered
1 small onion, sliced
1 package (12 ounces) bean
    sprouts
1 small carrot, julienne
½ cup chopped green onion
2 packages (12 ounces each)
    fresh chow fun noodles,
    cut into ½-inch strips

Seasonings:
2 teaspoons salt
1 teaspoon oyster sauce

Garnishes:
Chinese parsley
2 slices SPAM®, slivered
    (optional)

Stir-fry SPAM® in hot oil with vegetables for 1 to 2 minutes. Add noodles, salt, and oyster sauce; stir-fry additional minute or until noodles are heated through. Serve noodles on large platter; garnish with Chinese parsley and additional SPAM®, if desired.

Note: Chicken or beef broth may be used as gravy, if desired.

CHINESE

SPAM™ GAU GEE *(Meat Dumplings)*

Makes about 40

1 can SPAM®, minced
½ pound shrimp, shelled, cleaned,
    and minced
2 tablespoons minced green onion
2 tablespoons minced water chestnuts
1 teaspoon fresh ginger juice
¼ teaspoon salt
2 tablespoons soy sauce
1 tablespoon sesame oil
1 tablespoon sherry

Sweet-Sour Sauce:
⅓ cup sugar
¼ cup soy sauce
2 tablespoons sherry
2 tablespoons catsup
3 tablespoons vinegar
2 tablespoons cornstarch
1 cup water

1 package (50 count) won ton wrappers
Canola oil for deep frying

Mix together SPAM®, shrimp, green onion, water chestnuts, ginger juice, salt, soy sauce, sesame oil, and sherry in a bowl. Place a generous teaspoonful of mixture in middle of won ton wrapper. Moisten edges of wrapper; fold in half and press edges together to seal with mixture of cornstarch and water. Deep-fry in oil heated to 365°F until golden brown. Drain on absorbent paper and serve hot or at room temperature with Sweet-Sour Sauce, if desired.

Mix Sweet-Sour Sauce ingredients together in a saucepan; bring to a boil. Cook until sauce thickens; cool. Serve as dip with Gau Gee or Won Ton (see page 21).

SPAM™ TOAST

Makes about 4 dozen pieces

1 can SPAM®, finely minced or flaked
¼ cup raw Chinese fishcake
6 water chestnuts, finely minced
2 stalks green onion, minced

1 egg, beaten
1 teaspoon mirin (sweet rice wine)
12 slices bread, crust removed
Canola oil for frying

Combine SPAM®, fishcake, water chestnuts, green onion, egg, and mirin; mix well. Spread mixture on bread slices; cut each into fourths. Place slices, SPAM® side down, in oil heated to 365°F until edges begin to brown; turn and continue frying until golden. Drain on absorbent paper. Serve hot or at room temperature.

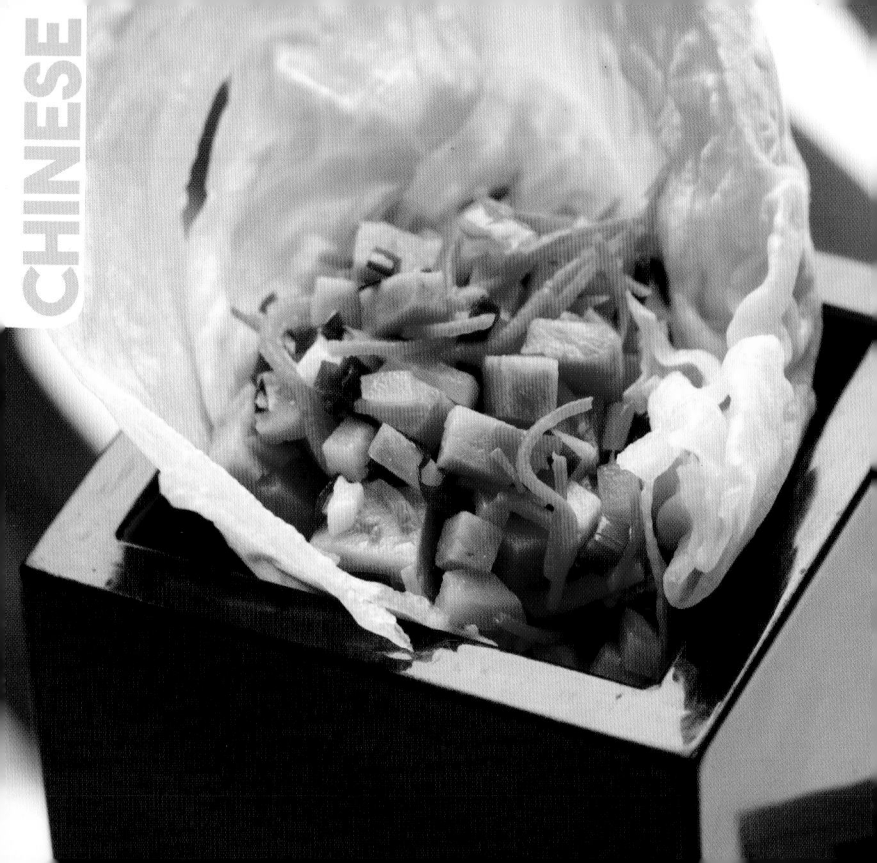

MINCED SPAM™ LETTUCE WRAP

Makes about 4 servings

1 can SPAM®, minced
½ teaspoon sugar
1 teaspoon cornstarch
2 teaspoons soy sauce
1 teaspoon mirin (sweet rice wine)
1 tablespoon water
1 teaspoon oil
1 teaspoon minced garlic

1 teaspoon minced fresh ginger
1 teaspoon sesame oil
¼ cup bamboo shoots, minced
3 dried mushrooms, soaked in warm water and chopped
¼ cup carrots, chopped fine
Lettuce leaves
Hoisin sauce

Combine SPAM®, sugar, cornstarch, soy sauce, mirin, and water; mix well and let stand 1 to 2 hours. Using a wok, heat oil and sauté the garlic and ginger; add marinated SPAM® and sauté until golden; remove from wok. Heat sesame oil and stir-fry bamboo shoots, mushrooms, and carrots 1 minute; return SPAM®; toss again and roll mixture in lettuce leaves to serve. Serve with Hoisin sauce as dip.

SPAM® WITH GREEN BEANS STIR-FRY

Makes about 4 servings

1 can SPAM®, cut into thin logs
1 clove garlic, minced
1 teaspoon oyster sauce
1 teaspoon cornstarch
3 tablespoons salad oil
2 cups green beans, cut into 2-inch lengths
½ cup sliced onion
¼ cup chicken broth
1 egg, slightly beaten

Mix together SPAM®, garlic, oyster sauce, and cornstarch; let stand 30 minutes. Heat 2 tablespoons of oil over high heat in wok; sear SPAM® slices and remove to warm plate. Add remaining tablespoon of oil to wok; stir-fry beans and onion 30 seconds. Add garlic marinade, broth, egg, and SPAM®. Cover and simmer 1 minute or until beans are cooked as desired. Serve hot over steamed rice.

SPAM™ FRIED RICE

Makes 6 to 8 servings

3 tablespoons salad oil
¼ pound shrimp, cleaned and minced
1¼ cups diced SPAM®
6 cups cold cooked rice

Seasonings:
2 tablespoons soy sauce
1 tablespoon oyster sauce
¼ teaspoon salt
2 eggs, beaten

Garnishes:
½ cup chopped green onion
2 slices SPAM®, slivered

Stir-fry shrimp and SPAM® in hot oil 1 to 2 minutes. Add rice and stir-fry additional 2 minutes or until rice is heated through. Add Seasonings and egg; cook additional minute while mixing and tossing gently until egg is cooked. Garnish with green onion and additional SPAM® to serve.

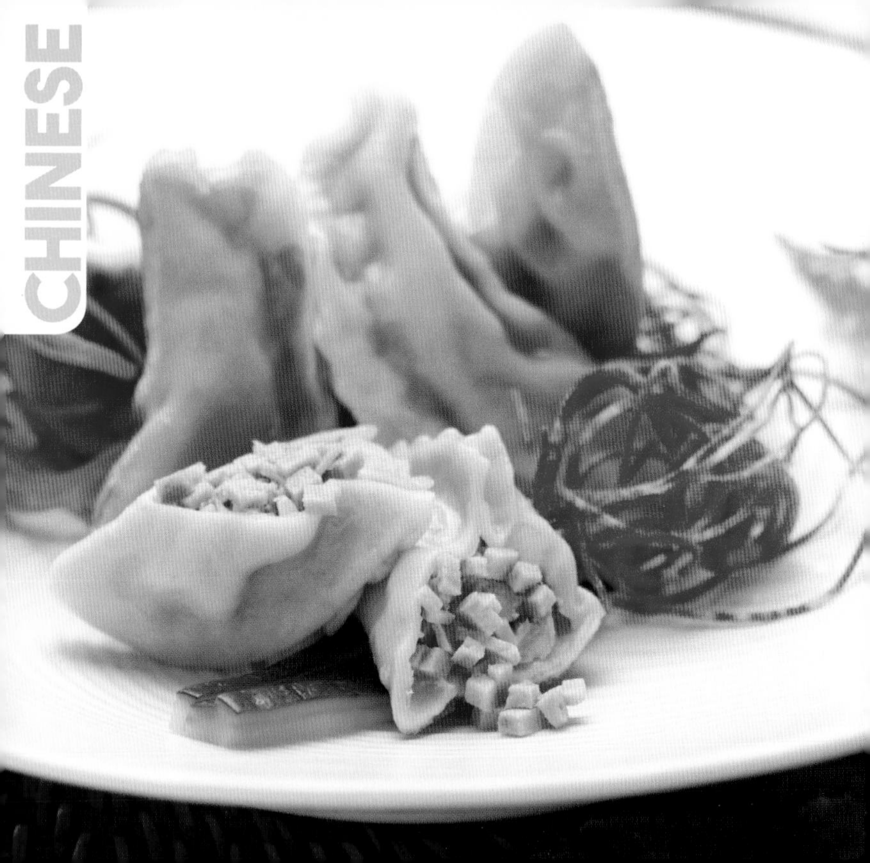

SPAM™ POT STICKERS

Makes about 24

¼ pound ground pork
1 can SPAM®, mashed
½ cup finely chopped Chinese (napa) cabbage
¼ cup green onion
1 teaspoon minced fresh ginger
1 clove garlic, minced
1 tablespoon soy sauce

1 tablespoon dry sherry
¼ teaspoon salt
24 round won ton or gyoza wrappers
2 tablespoons vegetable oil
1 cup chicken broth
Soy sauce, rice vinegar, and hot chili oil for dipping

In medium bowl, mix together ground pork, SPAM®, cabbage, green onion, ginger, garlic, soy sauce, sherry, and salt. Place 1 tablespoon filling in center of one wrapper; brush edges of wrapper with cold water. Bring edges of wrapper up to meet in center above filling; pinch and pleat closed. Repeat until all remaining wrappers are filled.

Heat oil in large nonstick skillet until hot; add dumplings, reduce heat to medium, and cook until undersides are browned, about 2 minutes. Add broth; cover tightly; boil until liquid is almost evaporated, about 5 to 8 minutes. Remove cover and continue cooking until liquid is completely evaporated. Serve immediately with guests making their own dipping sauce to taste with soy sauce, rice vinegar, and hot chili oil.

PIBIUM PAHB *(Korean Mixed Rice)*

Makes about 8 servings

12 cups hot cooked rice
1 can SPAM™ Kun Koki (see page 68), cut into thin strips
1 package (12 ounces) bean sprouts, washed and drained
1 bunch cooked watercress, cut into 1-inch lengths
1 cup purchased cabbage kim chee, drained and chopped
8 eggs, cooked as desired, optional

Sauce:
2 tablespoons sauce
2 tablespoons sesame seeds, crushed
1 teaspoon salad oil
1 teaspoon salt
1 teaspoon sugar

Cook bean sprouts and watercress in Sauce for 2 minutes; squeeze out excess liquid and set aside.

Rice Sauce:
1 tablespoon sesame seed oil
3 tablespoons soy sauce

Garnishes:
Fried egg strips, optional
Finely minced green onion

In large bowl, combine hot rice with SPAM® strips, seasoned watercress, bean sprouts, and kim chee. Pour Rice Sauce mixture over top of rice and toss gently until all ingredients are blended. Top with cooked egg (if used). Garnish with fried eggs strips and green onion to serve.

SPAM™ KUN KOKI *(Barbecued SPAM)*

Makes 4 to 6 servings

2 cans SPAM®, cut into 16 slices

Sauce:
3 tablespoons toasted sesame seeds
3 tablespoons salad oil
¼ cup soy sauce
⅓ cup finely chopped onion
¼ cup finely minced green onion
1 clove garlic, crushed
1 slice ginger, slivered
¼ teaspoon pepper
2 teaspoons sugar

Mix together Sauce ingredients; marinate SPAM® slices 30 to 60 minutes. Broil or pan-fry until both sides are browned. Best served hot with steamed rice.

SPAM™ JUHN *(Batter Fried SPAM®)*

Makes 4 to 6 servings

1 can SPAM®, sliced into 8
  pieces
1 cup flour

4 eggs, beaten
1 cup canola oil

Dredge SPAM® in flour, dip into eggs, again in flour and finally in beaten eggs. Pan-fry in hot oil until lightly browned, 1 to 2 minutes on each side. Drain on absorbent paper and serve with Ko Choo Jung Dipping Sauce.

KO CHOO JUNG DIPPING SAUCE *(Korean Hot Dip)*

Makes 1½ cups

½ cup soy sauce
3 tablespoons toasted sesame
  seeds
3 tablespoons ko choo jung
  sauce

½ cup vinegar
½ cup sugar
1 tablespoon minced green
  onion

Combine all ingredients in a jar; cover and shake vigorously. Serve with meat and vegetable dishes.

SPAM™ GOI CUON *(Summer Rolls)*

Makes 8 rolls

8 sheets bahn trang (rice paper wrappers)
1 cup warm water
4 lettuce leaves, cut in half
2 ounces long rice (vermicelli), cooked
½ cup shredded carrots
1 cup bean sprouts
½ cup mint leaves
8 to 12 pieces of SPAM® strips
1 to 2 stalks green onion, cut into 1-inch lengths

Nuoc Cham Sauce:
¼ cup sugar
½ cup water
⅓ cup wine vinegar
1 tablespoon nuoc man (fish sauce)
2 teaspoons ground red chili pepper
2 tablespoons shredded carrots
2 tablespoons chopped peanuts

Dip rice paper wrapper into warm water; quickly remove and lay flat on dry towel. Lay a piece of lettuce on the bottom third of the wrapper. Place 1 tablespoon long rice, 1 tablespoon carrots, few pieces of bean sprouts and mint leaves on top of the lettuce. Roll up the wrapper half-way to form a cylinder. Fold left and right sides of wrapper over the filling; arrange 2 pieces of SPAM® with green onions and continue rolling to seal. Keep covered with a damp towel until ready to serve. Serve with Nuoc Cham Sauce.

Mix together all ingredients for Nuoc Cham Sauce; serve as dip with Summer Rolls.

PAD THAI WITH SPAM® *(Fried Noodles)*

Makes 4 to 6 servings

½ pound rice noodles
¼ cup canola or vegetable oil
1 clove garlic, minced
1 egg, slightly beaten
1 can SPAM®,
   cut into matchstick pieces
¼ pound boneless chicken,
   sliced
¼ cup water, optional
3 tablespoons nam pla
   (fish sauce)

1 tablespoon sugar
1 tablespoon tamarind paste,
   optional
2 teaspoons vinegar
½ teaspoon chili powder,
   optional
1 tablespoon paprika
1 cup bean sprouts
¼ cup chopped roasted peanuts
1 stalk green onion, coarsely
   chopped

Garnishes:
Dried shrimps
Chopped roasted peanuts

Cilantro
Lime wedges

Soak noodles in warm water for 20 to 30 minutes or until softened; drain and set aside. Heat oil in wok on high heat; sauté garlic 1 minute. Stir in egg, SPAM®, and chicken; stir-fry 1 minute. Reduce heat and add noodles. Add nam pla, sugar, tamarind paste (if using), vinegar, chili powder (if using), and paprika; toss gently to combine. Mix in peanuts, half of bean sprouts, and green onions; stir-fry additional minute. When noodles are tender, transfer to warmed serving dish. Garnish with dried shrimps, peanuts, cilantro, lime wedges, and remaining bean sprouts and green onions.

Recipe Tip:
Tamarind trees are common in Hawai'i, recognizable for their long, dark pods. Tamarind paste, an optional ingredient in this recipe, is made from the fruit inside those pods. It's very sour and acidic. Find it in Asian groceries. Tamarind is one of the ingredients in Worcestershire sauce.

SOUTHEAST ASIAN

SPAM™ BAHN MI *(Vietnamese Sandwich)*

Makes 4 sandwiches

4 French rolls or croissants, sliced in
   half lengthwise
1 cup cooked SPAM®, shredded or cut
   into strips
2 small carrots, julienne
1 small turnip, julienne
1 small cucumber, sliced
1 small sweet onion, thinly sliced
1 bunch cilantro
Mayonnaise, optional
Hot garlic-chili pepper sauce, optional

Marinade:
⅓ cup rice vinegar
⅓ cup lime juice
6 tablespoons sugar
1½ teaspoons nuoc
   mam (fish sauce)
1 clove garlic, minced

Mix together Marinade ingredients; add carrots and turnips; marinate 4
to 5 hours. Drain well; set aside.

   Spread rolls with mayonnaise, if desired. Fill with SPAM®, then layer with marinated vegetables, slices of cucumber, onion, and a generous
amount of cilantro. Add a splash of hot garlic-chili sauce, if desired.

SPAM™ LUMPIA *(Spring Roll)*

Makes about 24 rolls

1 can SPAM®, grated
1 kamaboko, chopped fine
⅓ cup chopped green onion
1 package (12 ounces) bean
  sprouts, blanched
¼ cup coarsely grated carrot
24 lumpia (spring roll) wrappers
Canola oil for frying

Lumpia Sweet-Sour Sauce:
½ cup white vinegar
½ cup sugar
¼ cup catsup
1 cup water
1 tablespoon cornstarch
2 tablespoons water
Liquid hot sauce to taste,
  optional

Combine SPAM®, kamaboko, green onion, bean sprouts, and carrot; toss to mix thoroughly. Place 2 to 3 tablespoons of SPAM® mixture in center of each wrapper. Fold bottom corner over filling; tuck in two sides then top like an envelope. Moisten edges to seal. Pan-fry in hot oil until golden brown on all sides. Drain on absorbent paper and serve with Lumpia Sweet-Sour Sauce.

To prepare Lumpia Sweet-Sour Sauce, combine vinegar, sugar, catsup, and water in saucepan; bring to a boil. Mix cornstarch and water to make paste; add to hot mixture until of desired consistency; bring to a boil. If desired, add hot sauce just before serving.

SPAM™ PANCIT *(Fried Noodles)*

Makes 4 to 6 servings

1 package (8 ounces) pancit noodles
  (bijon or rice sticks)
3 tablespoons canola oil
2 cloves garlic, crushed
½ pound lean pork, cut in thin strips
1 piece boneless chicken breast, cut
  in thin strips
1 cup diced SPAM®
¼ pound shrimp, cleaned, and diced
½ cup chopped onion
1 small carrot, julienne
Salt and pepper to taste

Garnishes:
½ cup chopped green
  onion
3 limes, quartered
2 hard-cooked eggs,
  quartered

Dip:
Fresh lime juice
Soy sauce to taste

Soak noodles in cold water for 30 minutes or until soft. Sauté garlic in oil until lightly browned; remove. Add pork and sauté over medium heat, stirring frequently, 3 to 4 minutes. Add chicken and sauté 2 to 3 minutes. Add SPAM® and shrimp and sauté additional 2 to 3 minutes. Add onion, carrot, and seasonings; cook 1 to 2 minutes.

Drain rice noodles and cut into 4-inch lengths. Add to meat mixture and continue cooking, stirring frequently, until noodles are heated through, about 2 to 3 minutes. Place on large serving platter; sprinkle with green onion and arrange alternate wedges of lime and egg around. Serve hot with lime juice and soy sauce dip.

SPAM® AND POTATO QUICHE

Makes 4 to 6 servings

1 unbaked 9-inch pie crust
1 can SPAM®, minced
4 eggs
½ cup milk
2 cups frozen shredded hash brown potatoes, thawed
1 can (4.5 ounces) chopped green chilis, drained (optional)
2 cups (8 ounces) shredded 4-cheese blend

Bake pie crust in 9-inch glass pie pan at 425°F for 7 to 9 minutes or until light golden brown. Meanwhile, stir-fry SPAM® in medium skillet over medium heat 30 seconds; drain. Beat eggs in medium bowl; add milk, potatoes, and chilis; mix well.

Remove partially baked crust from oven; reduce oven temperature to 375°F. Sprinkle crust with 1 cup of the cheese; top with SPAM®, potato mixture, and remaining cheese. Return to oven and bake 40 to 50 minutes or until top is golden brown and knife inserted in center comes out clean. Cover edge of crust with strips of foil after 15 minutes of baking to prevent excessive browning. Let stand 5 minutes before cutting into wedges to serve.

SPAM™ LONG RICE

Makes 6 to 8 servings

1 bundle (4 ounces) long rice
   (cellophane noodle)
1 cup shredded SPAM®
1 quart beef or chicken broth
1 small slice fresh ginger root
2 teaspoons salt
¼ teaspoon white pepper
¼ cup chopped green onion

Soak long rice in warm water to cover and let stand 15 to 20 minutes; drain and cut into 4-inch lengths. Set aside.

Combine SPAM®, broth, ginger, salt, and pepper in saucepan with cover; bring to a boil. Add long rice and cook 10 to 15 minutes over low heat; mix in green onion. Serve hot or at room temperature.

OVEN KĀLUA SPAM™

Makes 6 to 8 servings

1 can SPAM®
1 ti leaf, washed and rib removed
1 tablespoon liquid smoke
Aluminum foil

Place SPAM® on ti leaves; sprinkle with liquid smoke. Overlap ti leaves to completely cover the SPAM®; tie securely with string. Wrap and seal in aluminum foil. Place wrapped SPAM® on rack in shallow roasting pan and roast at 350°F for 45 to 60 minutes. Slice and serve or shred SPAM® and let stand in mild brine solution with few drops liquid smoke, if desired.

Recipe tip:
To make brine solution, combine 1 tablespoon salt with 2 cups boiling water.

MEXICAN

SPAMISH™ RICE

Makes 4 to 6 servings

¼ cup canola oil
1 cup uncooked rice, washed and drained
1 can SPAM®, minced
¾ cup chopped onion
½ cup chopped green pepper
¼ cup celery
1 can (14 ounces) stewed tomatoes
1 cup water
1¼ teaspoon salt
1 teaspoon chili powder

Heat 2 tablespoons oil in large skillet; add rice and brown lightly, stirring frequently. Add remaining oil, SPAM®, onion, green pepper, and celery; cook until soft. Add remaining ingredients; cover and simmer 20 to 30 minutes over low heat until rice is tender.

Recipe tip:
If rice isn't sufficiently tender, add little more water; cover and continue to cook over low heat until soft.

SPAM™ BURRITOS

Makes 1 dozen small or 6 large burritos

1 cup chopped onion
1 tablespoon canola oil
1 can SPAM®, chopped
¼ pound lean ground beef
½ cup tomato sauce
1½ teaspoons chili powder
¼ teaspoon garlic powder
¼ teaspoon pepper
¼ teaspoon onion salt
1½ cups grated cheddar cheese
1 dozen small or 6 large flour tortillas

Sauté onion in hot oil until tender; add SPAM® and ground beef; cook until brown. Drain excess fat. Add tomato sauce, chili powder, garlic powder, pepper, and onion salt; simmer, uncovered, for 2 minutes. Set aside.

Heat tortillas on a warm griddle for a few seconds on each side. Place 1 to 2 tablespoons SPAM® mixture down center of each tortilla; sprinkle with cheese. Roll tightly and eat like a sandwich.

BREAKFAST QUESADILLAS

Makes 5 servings

10 (6- or 8-inch) flour tortillas
2 tablespoons vegetable oil
1½ cups shredded cheddar cheese
1 can SPAM®, shredded
5 eggs, cooked as desired
¾ cup purchased tomato salsa,
   optional

Lightly brush tortilla with oil or spray
large skillet with oil; heat in skillet about
5 seconds. Sprinkle on shredded cheese
and SPAM®, then top with egg. Brush
another tortilla with oil and place on
top of egg; cook 1 minute over low heat;
flip quesadilla over and cook additional minute or until heated through and
cheese melts. To serve, top each quesadilla with 1 to 2 tablespoons salsa, if
desired. Cut into wedges using a pizza
wheel or sharp knife.

MEXICAN

SPAM® CHILI

Makes about 4 servings

1 can SPAM®, coarsely ground
¼ cup minced onion
¼ cup chopped green pepper
2 cans (8 ounces each) tomato
   sauce

½ teaspoon salt
1 teaspoon sugar
1 tablespoon chili powder
1 can (15½ ounces) small red or
   kidney beans with liquid

Condiments:
Minced onions
Grated American cheese

Sauté SPAM®, onion, and green pepper together in non-stick saucepan. Add remaining ingredients; stir and simmer, stirring occasionally, until chili is of desired thickness, about 30 minutes over low heat. Sprinkle condiments over chili to serve. 'Ono with steamed rice or crackers!

Variation:
Cottage cheese and shredded Parmesan cheese may be substituted for cheddar or American cheese.

PORTUGUESE SPAM™ 'N BEANS SOUP

Makes 10 to 12 servings

2 ham shanks
1 package (12 ounces) Portuguese sausage, cut into ½-inch pieces
1 quart water
1 can SPAM®, cut into chunks
1 can (8 ounces) tomato sauce
1 large onion, wedged
2 potatoes, cubed
1 large carrot, cubed
1 small cabbage, chopped
2 cans (15 ounces each) red kidney beans including liquid
Salt and pepper to taste

Simmer ham shanks and Portuguese sausage in water for 2 hours over low heat. Add remaining ingredients; cook 15 to 20 minutes or until vegetables are cooked, adding more water if necessary. Season with salt and pepper to taste.

SPAM™ CAESAR SALAD

Makes 6 to 8 servings

Created at Caesar's Bar & Grill in Tijuana, Mexico, Caesar's famous salad has been acclaimed by epicures the world over. Here, it is topped with SPAM®.

1 clove garlic, crushed
⅔ cup olive oil
4 quarts romaine lettuce, chilled and torn
1 teaspoon salt
Freshly ground pepper
1 tablespoon Worcestershire sauce
1 egg, coddled 1 minute

¼ cup fresh squeezed lemon juice
2 tablespoons wine vinegar
4 anchovy fillets, chopped (optional)
½ cup grated Parmesan cheese
¾ cup croutons
1 cup SPAM® strips

Add garlic to oil; let stand overnight. Discard garlic. Place romaine in large, chilled salad bowl. Sprinkle with salt, pepper, and Worcestershire sauce. Break coddled egg into middle of salad; pour lemon juice and wine vinegar over egg; toss lightly to mix well. Add remaining ingredients except SPAM®; toss after each addition. Adjust seasonings if necessary. Sprinkle SPAM® strips over greens just before serving. Serve immediately.

SPAM™ PIZZA

Makes about 8 slices

1 purchased pizza crust
1 can (8 ounces) pizza sauce
1 can (4 ounces) sliced mushrooms, drained
2 cups shredded mozzarella, cheddar, or Monterey Jack cheese
¼ cup grated Parmesan or Romano cheese
1 can SPAM®, chopped

Prepare pizza crust as directed on package. Spread pizza sauce over partially baked crust. Sprinkle with mushrooms, cheese, and SPAM®. Bake at 425°F for 20 minutes or until cheese is melted and pizza is bubbly.

Variations:
- Add chopped bell peppers, chopped bacon, and/or ham

SPAM™ LASAGNE

Makes 6 to 8 servings

1 can SPAM®, coarsely grated
½ cup chopped onion
1 clove garlic, minced
1 tablespoon salad oil
2 cans (8 ounces each) tomato sauce
1 cup water
¾ teaspoon salt
½ teaspoon oregano

¼ teaspoon pepper
1 teaspoon sugar
1 ounce lasagne noodles, cooked per package directions and drained
2 cups shredded cheddar or American cheese
8 ounces sliced mozzarella cheese

Sauté SPAM®, onion, and garlic in hot oil 1 minute; add tomato sauce water, salt, oregano, pepper, and sugar. Cover and simmer 15 minutes over low heat.

Place half of noodles in bottom of lightly greased 13 × 3 × 9-inch baking dish. Spread half of cheddar or American cheese over noodles. Top with half of mozzarella cheese slices and half of the SPAM™ sauce. Repeat layers. Bake at 350°F for about 30 minutes or until cheese melts.

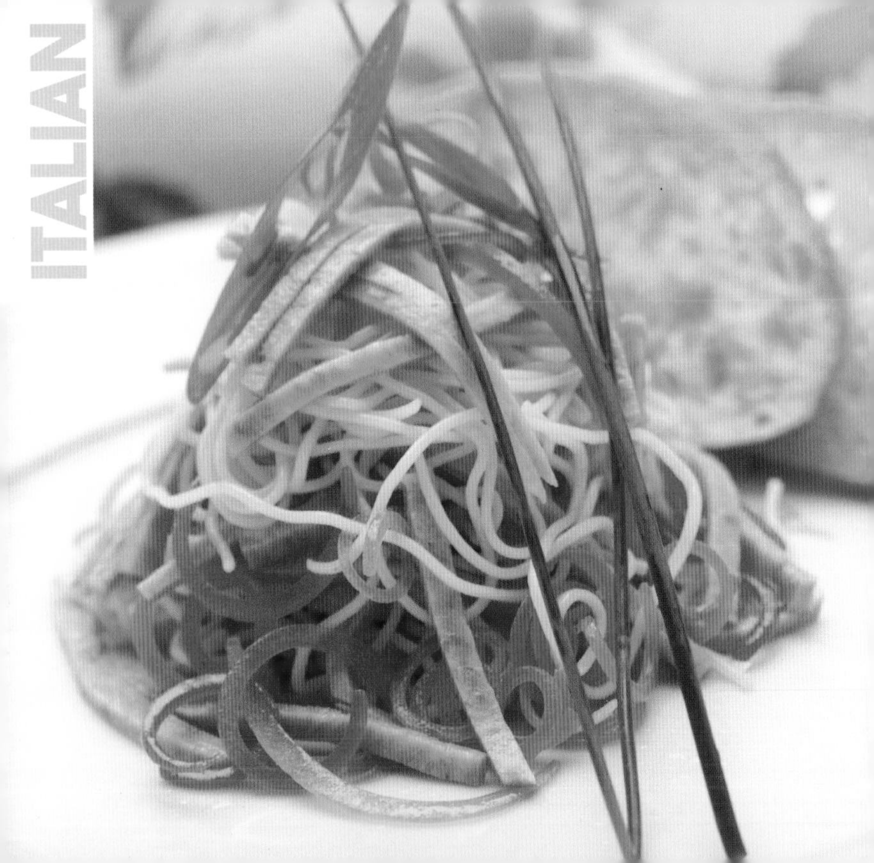
ITALIAN

SPAGHETTINI WITH SPAM®

Makes 4 to 6 servings

1 pound spaghettini or angel hair pasta
2 teaspoons minced garlic
½ cup olive oil
2 tablespoons minced cilantro
Crushed red pepper to taste, optional
1 can SPAM®, cut into strips
¼ cup lightly toasted unseasoned dry bread crumbs

Cook spaghettini or angel hair pasta until al dente according to package directions. Drain well and set aside.

Lightly brown garlic in olive oil in large saucepan. Add cilantro and crushed red pepper (if used) and stir; add SPAM® and cook over medium-high heat 1 minute. Toss SPAM® mixture with the pasta; add bread crumbs and toss again and serve immediately with garlic bread.

GLOSSARY

bahn trang: rice paper wrappers

Chinese parsley: cilantro

chow fun: flat Chinese noodle

daikon: Japanese name for large white radish

dashi-no-moto: Japanese instant soup granules

fried egg strips: fried egg cut into strips

furikake nori: seasoned Japanese seaweed mix

ginger: gnarled light brown root indispensable to Asian cooking

gon lo mein: stir-fried chow mein noodles

hoisin sauce: Chinese soybean sauce used for flavoring or as condiment

juhn: Korean term for food cooked in egg batter

kamaboko: steamed fishcake

kim chee: Korean hot, spicy preserved vegetables

ko choo jung: Korean hot sauce

long rice: translucent noodles made from mung beans

lumpia: Filipino spring roll with meat, vegetable, or fruit filling

lumpia wrapper: sheets of rice flour dough

mirin: sweet Japanese cooking rice wine

namasu: Japanese pickled vegetable dish

nam pla: Thai fish sauce

nori: Japanese name for dried seaweed sheets; aka laver

nuoc man: Vietnamese fish sauce

oyster sauce: Chinese oyster-flavored sauce

pancit/pansit: Filipino noodle dish

panko: Japanese name for bread crumbs

Portuguese sausage: spicy pork sausage

ramen: saimin noodles

saimin noodles: Japanese name for thin wheat or egg noodles

sake: Japanese rice wine

siu mai: Chinese steamed meat dumplings

somen: fine Japanese wheat flour noodles

soy sauce: seasoning made from roasted corn and steamed soybeans mixed with malt-mold, salt, and water, then fermented

tempura: Japanese fritters

teriyaki: soy-flavored Japanese sauce

wasabi: Japanese name for horseradish

water chestnuts: bulb of an Asian marsh plant

wun tun/won ton: Chinese meat dumplings